The High-Wheeler Race

Neville J. Barnard
Illustrated by Chantal Stewart

Contents

Chapter 1
The Meeting

Naomi was bored. Really bored.

The grown-ups had been talking for hours—125 minutes actually. Naomi was counting. And now it was 126 minutes. By the time Mrs. Amin stopped talking it would probably be 130 minutes. Dad had said it might be a long meeting, but Naomi didn't think it would be *this* long.

The meeting was at the new history museum. They were planning a race to advertise the official opening of the museum. They had decided on something unusual—a high-wheeler race. People would come from all over to see the old bikes race.

They had decided that ages ago, but still the meeting went on and on and on.

Naomi did what she always did when she was bored—she took her calculator out of her pocket and started tapping buttons. She loved to see the numbers dance across the screen as they flashed the answers to her questions.

Naomi was 2,555 days old when she was given her first calculator. She knew that because it was the first thing she figured out when she got the calculator. It was easy. At school, she learned that there are 365 days in a year. She got the calculator on her seventh birthday.

Months later, Naomi learned about leap years. Leap years happen every four years when February has an extra day. So she had to add the extra day. She calculated that she was really 2,556 days old when she got the calculator. And ever since then, she had been using it to help her figure things out.

Mrs. Amin was still talking. Naomi wondered how many words Mrs. Amin had spoken at the meeting. Then she wondered how many words had been spoken by everyone in all.

She decided to figure it out.

Someone was talking all the time. Naomi thought that one word was spoken every second. If she knew how many seconds had already passed, she would know how many words had been spoken.

Naomi tapped the buttons on the calculator. She couldn't believe what she saw on the screen. About 7,800 words had been spoken at the meeting already!

"It sure takes grown-ups a lot of words to plan one race," she thought.

Chapter 2
The Plan

Naomi was just about to estimate how long it might take to say one hundred thousand words, or even a *million* words, when she heard her father speaking. She looked up from her calculator.

"The race will start at the fountain at the end of Main Street," he said. "The riders will ride to the museum. That will count as one lap. Then they will ride back to the fountain. That will be the second lap. Then they'll ride back to the museum, and so on. Altogether, they will do ten laps. At the end of the tenth lap, the mayor will be at the museum waiting for the winner. Any questions?"

Naomi thought her father's explanation was very clear. But there were still twelve questions. Five of them were from Mrs. Amin, who must not have been paying attention.

As her father explained the plan again, Naomi thought about race day. Her father would be very busy. He had to make sure that first aid was available, and that the riders understood the rules.

The most exciting thing was that the race was going to be on TV! There was going to be a big TV screen on the clock tower. Naomi's father had to make sure the TV cameras were ready when the winner reached the finish line at the museum.

Most important of all, her dad had to make sure that the mayor was at the finish line to greet the winner.

Finally everyone, even Mrs. Amin, agreed that the plan was great. Nothing could possibly go wrong. They ended the meeting at last.

Chapter 3
The Mistake

It was the day of the big race! Naomi went along with her dad to watch. They got there early so that he could check that everything was in place.

While Naomi was waiting for the race to begin, she took out her calculator.

What Naomi liked most about her dad's race plan was that there would be ten laps. Ten was her favorite number. It was the very first number that she had to press two different buttons on the calculator to make! She thought that made it pretty special.

It was great to watch as the 10s turned into 100s which turned into 1000s—just by pressing the multiply button again and again and again. All those wonderful zeros!

The race was going to be a lot of fun. People could watch all the old bicycles race by from either side of the street. And with a TV screen at the clock tower, everyone would be able to clearly see the finish of the race at the museum.

"At the museum?" Naomi thought. "Uh oh!"

Suddenly she realized that her father had made a terrible mistake! Something was going to go wrong, and it all had to do with her favorite number. "Dad," Naomi called out, "you've made a mistake! Ten's an even number!"

"Yes, I know that," said her father, smiling. "And I'm glad you do too."

"But don't you see? The mayor will be at an odd number!" Naomi protested.

"What are you talking about?" asked her dad.

"The number of laps is even!" Naomi explained. "So the mayor needs to change ends!"

"What do you mean, *change ends*?" he asked.

"Look," said Naomi, as she pointed to her dad's map of the race course.

"The race is starting here, at the fountain. The mayor will be waiting at the museum. Right?" she asked.

Her father nodded.

"But one lap gets the riders to the museum. After two laps, they're back here at the fountain," she continued. "So three gets them back to the museum, and four gets them back here again. See?"

Naomi looked at her father. He just shook his head. "So?" he asked.

"The race is ten laps long. That's an even number. It's going to end back at the starting line—the fountain. Not at the museum. So the mayor needs to be right here at at the fountain!"

Naomi's dad was quiet for a moment. Then he patted her head the way he did when he was really pleased with her.

"You know, Naomi, even a calculator wouldn't have picked up that mistake. You really do know your numbers," he said.

Dad looked at his watch, and the smile faded from his face. It was almost time for the race to start, and the mayor was in the wrong place!

Chapter 4
The Race

"Ready, set, go!" a voice shouted. The race had begun!

"Don't worry," said Naomi. "Give the mayor a call on his cell phone. He'll have plenty of time to walk down here to the finish line."

Dad smiled. Then he quickly dialed the mayor's number.

But right away the smile disappeared.

"His phone is turned off," Dad said. "I can't contact him!"

"Don't worry," said Naomi. "I'll just run to the museum and ask him to come down here."

Her father just shook his head.

"It will never work. There are too many people and you can't get in the way of the riders! But we've got to get a message to the mayor somehow!"

Naomi looked around the street. There were huge crowds of people everywhere. Dad was right.

She could never get to the mayor in time with so many people in the way. What could they do?

Naomi looked around again. Then she saw it!

"Dad," she said, "where is the big TV screen controlled from?"

"That van over there," he replied. "Why?"

Naomi scribbled a note on a piece of paper. "Tell them to flash this on the screen!" Her father read the note, smiled, and ran to the van.

Soon some words flashed on the screen. URGENT MESSAGE TO MAYOR. CHANGE OF PLAN. COME TO STARTING LINE.

"I hope he can read it from way up at the museum," thought Naomi.

25

The race continued. Lap two became lap three. Lap four melted into lap five. Still there was no sign of the mayor. Lap six was over. Lap seven was completed. Lap eight was finished. Where was the mayor? Lap nine was over. Lap ten started.

Soon the first bike was only a block away. The race would be over any second. Where was the mayor?

Naomi looked around to find her father. He was standing near the fountain. And standing next to him was the mayor! He had made it!

Just then a tall man in a black and white striped top rode his high-wheeler across the line. He had won the race! The mayor put a yellow sash over his shoulders and shook his hand. Everything had worked out after all— and it was all thanks to Naomi.

As the crowds started to drift away, Naomi's father came over to her.

"Thanks to you, the race was a success!" he said as he gave her a big hug. "Have I ever told you how much I love you?"

Naomi whipped the calculator from her pocket. "At least once every day for eight and a half years," she replied. She tapped some buttons.

Eight years = 365 x 8 = 2,920 days
Half a year = about 182 days
Two leap years = 2 days
2,920 + 182 + 2 = 3,104

"I'd estimate about 3,104 times," she said with a grin. "But Dad, even that's not enough!"

Solving Math Problems

There are many different ways to solve math problems. You can use a calculator to solve problems that are hard to figure out in your head. You can use pencil and paper. Sometimes simple problems are easier and faster to solve in your head! You can also estimate to solve some problems.

Every math problem is different. You need to decide the best way to solve each problem.

A calculator is a useful tool.

High-Wheeler Bicycles

A high-wheeler is a kind of bicycle that was popular long ago, in the 1880s. It was one of the first bicycles.

High-wheelers are difficult to ride. The seat is above the large front wheel. This means the rider's feet can't touch the ground! And a high-wheeler has no brakes. The rider has to pedal backward to slow down and stop.

Today, some high-wheeler bicycles are in museums. High-wheelers are also used for special events, like parades or races.

These people are racing on high-wheeler bicycles.

Think About the Story

In *The High-Wheeler Race*, Naomi loves to figure things out. Think about these questions.

- What kinds of things does Naomi like to figure out?
- Why does she use a calculator?
- What mistake does Naomi's dad make when he plans the race? How does Naomi help him fix the mistake?

To learn more about numbers and solving math problems, read the books below.

SUGGESTED READING
Windows on Literacy
Numbers and You
Race Day

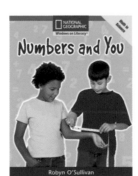

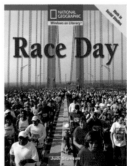